PowerPrinciples

Do you have the Winning Edge?

"The highest IQ or all the formal education in the world will not make you successful without the PowerPrinciples."

Ed Hall, President and CEO, Hall Associates

"I believe that advice on subjects like this are best delivered by those who have lived the subject matter. Jeb Blount has lived the subject matter as a successful Sales Professional, leader, and coach. This book is a great combination of personal stories and sound advice that REALLY WORKS. Once you have read it you will find yourself rereading the book for the details you missed the first time...and the second time...and the third time. This is a book that should be reread at least once a year for as long as you are involved in growing a business or your career."

Ed Evans, Executive Vice President, Human Resources and Organizational Development, Allied Waste

"Taking what is elusive and difficult and making it clear to everyone is a skill that is rare. Jeb has done just that. Power Principles is fantastic. If you are serious about winning, read this book."

Dr. Bill Sutton, Associate Director and Professor, DeVos Sport Business Management Program, University of Central Florida, Former Vice President of Team Marketing, National Basketball Association

ADVANCE PRAISE FOR POWERPRINCIPLES

"PowerPrinciples is required reading for Sales Professionals, Business Leaders and any one else who dreams of accomplishing great things in life."

Paul Smith, Vice President of Sales, Peak Performance

"Jeb Blount has laid out in PowerPrinciples, a proven and attainable method for not only winning, but winning big, and winning consistently. His down-to-earth writing style makes it easy to grasp his principles for success and incorporate them in to your life. This book is a must read for anyone who wants to be the best they can be in life. Where was this book when I was starting out?"

Brad Sonday, President and CEO, Summit Executive Recruiters

"Jeb's personal stories and his strong and passionate writing style make this a compelling read that will compel you to take action to live your dreams"

Deborah Koch, Senior Vice President of Marketing, Gibraltar Private

"DO NOT READ THIS BOOK unless you are fully committed to becoming a winner. If you are, waste no time because the walk of a winner is a great journey."

Cyndi Gundy, Instructor, University of Central Florida, School of Business, Head Coach, UCF National Collegiate Sales Competition Team

"Well done, finally a sales book that teaches and inspires."

Larry Hake, Regional Vice President of Sales, Allied Waste

ADVANCE PRAISE FOR POWERPRINCIPLES

"Jeb Blount is the real deal. By applying the five PowerPrinciples, his team was the first and only sales team, in the history of his Fortune 500 corporation, to earn the President's Award. Wow! His PowerPrinciples can do the same for you - in your work AND your life. Be savvy; buy this book, put it to use, and get ready to celebrate the victories and successes of your dreams!"

Michelle Nichols, Savvy Selling columnist and Podcast host for BusinessWeek.com, www.savvyselling.com

"PowerPrinciples is the one sales book everyone should read. Business professionals in all disciplines will benefit from Jeb's powerful message!"

Emily M. Campbell, PMP, Sr. Project Manager, Engineering, LexisNexis® Risk & Information Analytics Group Seisint Inc.

"Jeb Blount's PowerPrinciples will make you into a powerful source of sales excellence. He simplifies and makes practical the principles that drive salespeople to great success. A must read!"

Jeff Lehman, author, The Sales Manager's MENTOR, 2nd Edition

"I personally witnessed the immediate, positive changes that Jeb's PowerPrinciples made in my sales team. If you want to change your sales results, buy a copy for every sales professional and sales leader in your organization today!"

Chris Dods, Division Vice President, Environmental Services Division, PSC

PowerPrinciples

Do you have the winning edge?

Jeb Blount

Palm Tree Press
Orlando

Palm Tree Press
10151 University Blvd.
Suite 270
Orlando, Florida 32817

Published by Palm Tree Press
Printed in the United States of America

Cover Design:
David Stanfill
www.sayitontheweb.com
Jean Bersch
www.thesetup.com

First Edition

Library of Congress Control Number: 2007925946

ISBN-13: 978-0-9794416-1-5
ISBN-10: 0-9794416-1-7

**In memory of my Grandfathers,
James Beaton and Edward Blount.**

*You taught me that work ethic is a virtue
and showed me the beauty of big dreams.*

TABLE OF CONTENTS

FOREWORD

I grew up the youngest of four children, living a normal middle class American life. Despite all the hallmarks of a good life - a college degree, nice job, happy family - I lived a beige existence. I fit right into the middle class mold, blending into the crowd, even though a voice deep inside of me screamed that I was different and that this beige lifestyle just didn't fit. Then one day I met a person who saw something in me that to everyone else was invisible. He would splash neon paint all over my beige world, revealing the purpose and path I was born to take.

In the summer of 2000, I was working for one of the largest early childhood education companies in the country as a corporate trainer. The enrollment in our 600 schools had been shrinking and our CEO brought in a consultant to help us reverse the trend. All of the corporate trainers had been summoned to Miami, Florida to meet with this consultant. We were going to attend a three day train the trainer course to learn to teach our school directors a new methodology for "selling" the empty spaces in their schools.

A week before this meeting my father died suddenly. It was devastating. With his death, I found myself analyzing my own life and my future. I almost didn't go to Miami but, for some reason, I found the will, and I got on that airplane. Sad, confused and soul searching I sat in my hotel room the night before the meeting dreading the next day. I was expecting the typical training session - a boring day spent listening to an overpaid consultant with a fancy slide show, a big ego, and a huge training handbook.

I slowly dragged myself to the meeting room the next morning, still expecting the worst. I could see the same trepidation on faces of the other trainers in the room. The next thing I remember this fast talking, passionate, ball of energy exploded into the room. He had a big smile on his face as he told us to hold on tight because we were going to have fun. The energy in the room changed instantly. For a moment I felt like I had entered the twilight zone. Our company of sensible-shoe-wearing educators would never be the same!

He informed us that we were going to learn how to teach our school directors to sell. Instantly the walls went up. We knew nothing about sales. To me, sales was something for glad-handing men, in polyester suits, with slick pitches. I was a teacher who taught other teachers. Teachers didn't sell!

The next two days forever changed me. My mind was stretched, I was challenged, I learned, I grew. I had never met anyone like Jeb Blount. He was so confident and so passionate about teaching and coaching us. He was unrelenting in demanding results and perfection. He stopped us when we made mistakes and made us do it over and over until it was right. Overcoming our beliefs and mental roadblocks about selling was daunting. Several of the sensible shoe girls threatened to quit! Jeb was unmoved. He kept reassuring us that we could do it. His energy was infectious and we stuck with it.

In the end I was transformed. I was more confident. I stood taller. Jeb pushed us to succeed. He refused to accept beige behavior. I left that meeting seeing the world differently, seeing myself differently. I felt more alive, more passionate. I threw away my sensible shoes and bought high heels and flip flops.

Jeb changed my life. He pushed and he demanded because he cared. He saw potential in me. He became my coach. He opened doors for me that I never knew existed. Suddenly I was transformed from a trainer to a Sales Professional. He indoctrinated me with his *PowerPrinciples*, providing me with a clear formula for success.

Today, I have a display case full of awards and I have made more money than I could have ever fathomed as an educator. I have seen my goals fulfilled and dreams realized. He is my mentor and my lifetime friend. He was born to share this incredible gift and to inspire change in the lives of others. Open your heart, embrace change, and use Jeb's *PowerPrinciples* to help you make your dreams come true.

Jodi Bagwell
Raleigh, North Carolina
January, 2007

INTRODUCTION

From the Author

The Sales Addiction

> *"I had no idea how to sell, but I remember deciding that no matter what, I was going to make my quota..."*

The First Taste

During the winter of my junior year in high school I, along with all of the other juniors in my school, went through the chore of choosing our senior year classes. I was looking forward to my senior year. I planned to have fun. For three years I'd done my duty. I had been a good student, taken my requisite classes and worked hard. My senior year was going to be a breeze. Soccer team, golf team, parties, prom, and easy classes. I signed up for anything that I thought would get me out of studying. Just sit back, relax, and enjoy...

One of the "easy" classes I chose was Yearbook. I didn't think there would be much homework and it sounded like it would be easy to just coast through. There were also a lot of girls on the Yearbook staff and I figured that would be a bonus. There would even be regular planning meetings, which would get me legally out of class during the spring of my junior year. Could there be a better way to earn credits?

My First Quota

At the first Yearbook meeting our teacher, Mrs. Shearouse, made an announcement. It was time to sell advertisements. All around me I heard groans. The veterans on the Yearbook staff made it clear that selling was something they did not like to do. She gave us a price list, a pep talk, and a $200 sales quota. Then sent us on our way. So began my first taste of sales.

I had no idea what to do and no idea how to sell but remember deciding that no matter what, I was going to make my quota as soon as possible. I wanted to waste no time getting back to goofing off. I got started by going around my town and asking local merchants to place an ad. It didn't take long to start making sales. In fact, I exceeded my quota in the first three days. It was actually fun and I couldn't believe how addictive it was. So instead of packing up and going home, after I hit my quota, I just kept going. Every day after school I hit the streets and made sales calls. Once I had called on every business in my town, I moved to the next town, and eventually to a bigger city nearby. The sales kept coming and I just kept going out every day. I loved the feeling I got each time I made a sale. My parents were convinced that I had lost my mind.

Judgment Day

A month later, Mrs. Shearouse called a meeting at which we were to turn in our ad sales. She went around the room and asked each individual what they had sold. The results were dismal. Most people had not made their quota and none had managed to sell more than $300. When she finally came to me, I couldn't help smiling while announcing that I had sold $3,700 in Yearbook advertisements. I could see the disbelief on the faces of my classmates. However, disbelief turned to awe when I handed over the orders and the checks. It was an incredible feeling. I knew right then and there that I was addicted to sales.

After the meeting was over Mrs. Shearouse asked if I would stick around for a moment. When everyone had gone, she delivered the news. Because I worked so hard on the ad sales she was making me Editor of the Yearbook. I couldn't believe it! She was choosing me over talented people who had been working on the Yearbook since their freshman year. These students deserved the Editor position. They had worked for it, knew how to do it and were expecting to get the promotion. Instead, she chose me, the person who sold the most ads, to be the Editor. And, even though my intent had been to find an easy class, the hard work of being Yearbook Editor turned out to be one of the most rewarding experiences of my life.

Real Rewards

I learned a valuable lesson: *the real rewards, in business and life, always go to those who sell.* Later, after I chose sales as my profession, I came to understand the rewards a career in sales offers. Sales people have the most lucrative jobs in business today. We make more money and have more fun than anyone else and, unlike most people, we are in control of our own destinies. Because we are in sales, we look at our goals for our lives and careers and we know that we have the power to achieve them. There are few careers that offer these opportunities. In sales, income and success are in direct correlation to effort.

Sales Professionals...

- are the highest paid professionals in business;
- are more challenged and happier in their jobs;
- have more freedom and more flexibility;
- have more control of their income and goals;
- reap all of the rewards: recognition, trips, cash.

www.SalesGravy.com

"I had it in my heart. I believed in myself, and I had confidence. I knew how to do it, had natural talent and pursued it."
- Muhammad Ali

The Big Three

Before moving on I must level with you. To be successful at selling you must have a passion for it. Some would call it an addiction. If you are reading this book trying to find inspiration that will cause you to actually like a sales career you hate, I recommend you consider another line of work. No book, no training, no speaker will make you like sales if sales is not for you. If it is not your calling, go do something else you love because there is no benefit in wasting precious time working at something that does not make you happy.

Sales success is, and always will be, an equation of three things: **Talent + Skill + Desire**. I write this book assuming that you possess talent for sales and you are in a sales job where you can leverage your talent. I am assuming that you have skills and are gaining new skills that allow you to put your talents, as a Sales Professional, to work. I assume that you have the desire and drive to be your best.

Despite what many gurus on sales and motivation will tell you, there are no substitutes for these three essential ingredients. If you are addicted to sales, if you wake up every day and you can't wait to hit the streets, keep reading.

Not The Typical Sales Book

Normally when you read a sales book, you learn about the power of prospecting, getting to the decision maker, listening, questioning, presenting, positioning, closing and so on. I hope you are reading as many books that address these important selling skills as you can get your hands on. These skills and many more are the core of a great sales career. I've studied, practiced and honed them over my career and so should you.

This book does not focus on selling skills. Instead, it is designed to help you learn how to better leverage your talents, skills, and master your desire. The information in this book will not replace what you already know about sales and how to succeed in your field or industry. It will, however, help you Power Up to get the success you deserve, to achieve your goals, and fulfill your dreams. The *PowerPrinciples* put into action, will help you take full advantage of your sales career to bring abundance and success to your life.

The Winning Edge

Over my 20 years in the sales profession as a Sales Professional, Sales Manager, and a Senior Executive with a Fortune 500 company, I've had the privilege of working with and learning from some of the most successful people in the world. These individuals have maximized success in almost every area of their lives, accomplishing what most people only dream about, and accumulating significant wealth along the way. Through my interactions with these talented, driven people, I discovered five *PowerPrinciples* that were critical to their ultimate success in achieving their goals.

Most of us spend a lifetime working to get the things we want. Some of us succeed and some of us don't. That's the way life is. Even the best and brightest among us sometimes fail to achieve goals, hit targets and make dreams become reality. Some people, however, have improved their probability of success by consistently employing these *PowerPrinciples* to gain the Winning Edge.

The PowerPrinciples

**Define What You Want and Write It Down
Invest In Yourself
A Little Bit Every Day
Get A Coach
Take Action**

"Common sense is not so common."
Voltaire

The PowerPrinciples Work!

Do you have the Winning Edge? I wrote this book because I want you to get the success you deserve. I love the sales profession and the hardworking sales people who give so much of themselves to keep the wheels of commerce turning. You were born to win and you have the power to get what you want out of life.

The five *PowerPrinciples* are proven and in many ways, simple common sense. Successful people have employed these strategies for centuries. Achieving your goals and dreams is a serious responsibility. Life will not wait for you. When you put these *PowerPrinciples* to work, you will gain the Winning Edge and guarantee a lifetime of turning dreams into reality. Take action now. Turn the page, take notes, and dream big!

Define What You Want
and
Write It Down

> *"I clearly remember the moment that everything clicked for David. It was the day he finally connected the dots between clearly defined goals and success."*

The City of Lights

The day I became a Sales Manager was both joyous and terrifying. I had been campaigning for the position for months and, as a last resort, had threatened to quit if I didn't get the job. Then it was official, I'd been promoted, but the thrill wore off quickly with the news that I had inherited the worst performing sales team in the company. The "Bad News Bears" could have out-played these guys. Reality sunk in. I had traded a very nice six figure income as a Sales Professional for a new city, less money, and the worst sales team in the company. What was I thinking?

On my first official day as a Sales Manager, I met David. He picked me up at the airport. I'd already been given an ear full about him from the Vice President of my Region, who had called the day before to congratulate me on my promotion and demand that I fire David. As we walked out of the airport terminal, I was preparing for the worst.

David's sales performance was mediocre and he was way behind his quota. He had come up through the ranks and had been a truck driver before somehow managing to land a job in sales. He had no formal sales training, no guidance, no direction, and he lacked polish. However, he was smart enough to know he needed help. The first thing he said when we got into his car at the airport was, "Boss, I don't know how to sell like you, I've been losing some big accounts lately, and I need help. Will you please teach me?"

David was eager to learn everything and anything. He had a natural talent for sales and a big heart. He worked harder than anyone else. He was persistent, resilient, driven, and diligently developed new sales skills. It wasn't long before he was delivering better numbers. With his improving sales productivity came bigger commission checks.

Connecting The Dots

I clearly remember the moment that everything clicked for David. It was the day he finally connected the dots between clearly defined goals and success. That day he began his journey across the line between merely existing and living his dreams. That morning we were having breakfast and talking about his upcoming sales day. When he had finished giving me the run down on the calls we would be making, I changed the subject and asked, "David, what do you want?"

I'm sure he had never been asked that question before because his reaction was like a deer in headlights. I explained that his talent for selling would open doors for him like never before. If he was going to take advantage of these opportunities, he needed to know what he wanted so that he could build a road-map for achievement. It was time for David to point to the stands and call his home runs.

We spent the next few weeks discussing his goals. Through a series of talks I learned that David had a young family and was living in a dangerous neighborhood with poor schools. David had only one desire, and that was to get his family out. He just didn't have a plan. His sincerity and devotion to his family touched me deeply and I became determined to help him change his life.

David began the process of committing his goals to paper: a new house in a good neighborhood, a needed vacation for his family and secured college funding for his children. He also had a very special dream. He wanted to take his wife to Paris. There had been no money when they were first married and David, ever the devoted husband, wanted to give his wife the honeymoon she never had.

We figured out how much he would have to make in commissions to accomplish his goals. Then, based on his financial goals, we created a step by step plan that we called his *Steps to Success*. We set targets for cold calls, first time appointments, follow-up appointments, presentations, and the number of deals he would have to close each week, each month, each quarter and for the year. We mapped it all out on a piece of paper which would, in time, become the basis for the *PowerPrinciples Goal Sheet*™.

It Was Magic!

If you ask David about this today he'll say, "It was just like magic. Once I put those goals on paper everything started changing for me."

He was so proud to show me his new house. I marveled at the change in his life as his kids played in their new swimming pool. His sales career had taken off and he was reaping the rewards. There were no more calls for his head from our Vice President because David was at the top of the sales rankings.

Recently he built his dream home in Florida. His kids are almost grown and he is putting them through college. David was named Sales Manager of the Year for a prestigeous Fortune 500 company, and has built one of the most successful sales teams in his organization's history. Money is no longer an issue for David but he still sits down and sets goals that keep moving him foward towards his dreams.

Defining Moments

In just over a year, David and the team I inherited, had moved from last place to first place in the sales rankings. As a reward I was promoted and moved to California. One day, almost two years later, David called to say that he was flying out to LA and needed to talk.

We went to dinner and caught up on our families and careers. Toward the end of dinner he looked over at me and said, "Boss, I want to tell you why I came to see you. I'm sure, as busy as you are, that you don't even remember this but, do you recall when I set that goal to take my wife to Paris?"

I quickly nodded yes.

"We took that trip and it was incredible. I can't begin to tell you how it made me feel. When we were walking through Paris, holding hands, all the guilt I had for not taking her on a honeymoon when we were first married went away. If it wasn't for you pushing me to set goals this would never have happened and I came here to thank you." That was a defining moment in my life. The book you are reading was born that evening.

"A written goal is motivation's playing field."
- Jeb Blount

What Do You Want?

You want something. You have goals. You have dreams. The reason I know that you have dreams and goals is that as a Sales Professional, it's just in your nature. It is likely that you chose sales as your profession because you recognize that no other career in business today offers more opportunities for achievement and success.

As individuals our goals and dreams are unique. For some of you, what you want can be complex and for others extremely simple. Some of you want bigger homes, financial independence or cool toys. Others want to put their kids through college without going broke or have more time to spend with them while they are little. Some of you are looking for better personal relationships, career advancement or more money.

What matters most is that you find a way to get what you want, and that you leverage your talents to make your dreams come true. You are no different than David or any of the other successful sales people I've met over the years. Just like them, *you deserve to win.*

The Most Important Question

The question I asked David is the same one I ask every Sales Professional I meet, *"What do you want?"* I use this question to encourage conversation and inspire contemplation. Understanding what people want is the most basic starting point for any relationship.

What's sad to me, is how few of us actually take time to think about what we really want. I don't mean just a passing thought. I mean a serious conversation with ourselves during which we make tough, clear decisions about what is most important, what dreams are priorities, what goals we must achieve, and what really motivates us in life.

When I ask this simple question, *"What do you want?"* the answers most often returned are: "I just want to be happy" or "I want to be successful." Most people say that they want to be the best on their team and win the respect of their peers - often without defining what that means and the steps they'll have to take to be "the best". Some people just say "I don't know", which is an honest answer though not the optimal way to journey through life.

So I dig a little deeper and ask questions like, "What does happy mean to you?", "How do you define success?" or "How will you become the #1 sales person on your team?" The subsequent blank stare tells me we have a lot of work to do.

Practice and Patience

Defining what you want will not be easy. It will take practice and patience. Get some help from your significant other, your friends, manager or a coach; they can provide you with perspective and feedback that will help you be honest with yourself.

Of course, the most important thing you can do is start! A written goal is motivation's playing field. When you write down your goals you turn energy into action. Action is motion. Motion creates momentum. Momentum moves you forward towards your dreams.

Epiphany

Back in my mid-twenties, I was out on the street selling just like you - knocking on doors, working hard in my territory to build my sales career and cash some commission checks. I wore out many pairs of shoes but enjoyed the freedom and flexibility of my sales job. I was hitting some home runs and I loved the winning feeling I got after closing a deal. I lived for the kill! Even better, I was working for a great company and people were starting to notice my success.

I remember the day when I had an epiphany that changed my life. That particular morning I had closed the biggest deal of my life and was flying higher than a kite. My managers were calling to congratulate me but there was no time to talk because I was on my way to close another one. I had a prospect who had been putting off a decision and my plan was to walk into his office confidently and get a signature. (*I have a core philosophy that the best time to get your next sale is right after you've just closed your last one.*) On that day, I was on fire, and nothing could stop me!

One of the habits I formed early in my career was always listening to audio programs in my car when I was out selling. One of the audio programs I enjoyed listening to was Zig Ziglar's goal setting. I'd listened to it a dozen times. I don't know if it was the adrenaline, the realization that with the big sale I was now a player in my organization, or divine providence, but that morning, for the first time, the lessons were finally sinking in.

I realized that I had no plan for my future. Nothing! I had some vague ideas but had never really defined my path. I had no goals other than to close the next deal and had never given serious thought to what I really wanted.

Taking Action

After putting the seal on a successful day, I stopped at an office supply store and bought a composition notebook. On my way home I pulled over at a rest stop on the Blue Ridge Parkway, sat down under a big tree and started thinking. It was a lot harder to clearly define what I wanted than I thought it would be. I had to work at it, and work at it, and work at it! The more I practiced, the easier it became. That day and over the weeks that followed, I wrote down my goals in the notebook I'd bought. Looking back, it is simply amazing how the goals I wrote down shaped the next ten years of my life.

That afternoon, I decided that the one thing I wanted in my personal life more than anything else was a home on the water, with a dock where I could park a big boat. For me, that was the ultimate dream, the one thing that would define "arrival." It took ten years of hard work but I eventually purchased a beautiful home on the water in Southwest Florida, and today my boat "Sea Monkey" is at my dock.

The work I had to do to make my dream come true helped me deliver great value to the companies I worked for. In fact, after writing down my goals, I set my company's all-time record for the most sales in a single year - a record that went unbroken for ten years. It was a huge accomplishment for a Sales Professional working in a Fortune 500 company with hundreds of sales people. That dream was my fire. It burned hot when things were going well and fanned the flames when I was down.

Today I have new dreams that shape my motivation and, I am reminded of the power of written goals each morning when I walk out into my backyard at sunrise, stand on my dock, and watch the dolphins play.

Some People Know

Some Sales Professionals have defined exactly what they want. They have a road map for their lives and it is always written down. Because they have written goals, these winning Sales Professionals have a much higher probability of achieving their goals.

I have no doubt that you know some of these winners. It is likely, in conversations with your friends or colleagues, you have described them as successful or lucky. The conversation sounds something like this, "Everything always seems to go right for John. He is so lucky" or "Amy has everything going for her, no matter what happens she comes out on top."

If you were to ask John or Amy, you'd quickly find that they have a clearly defined path. You would find that they have goals that are written down and you'd find that they know exactly what they want. You would also discover that not everything is perfect. They hit rough water just like everyone else. However, because they have, written goals and a plan, they stay on course even in stormy seas.

"Winners can tell you where they are go-ing, what they plan to do along the way, and who will be sharing the adventure with them." - Dennis Watley

Forks In The Road

"You Can't Always Get What You Want" - a great Stones song and so true. I must level with you: just because you define what you want and write it down doesn't mean that you will always get it. You just greatly increase your probability.

You won't achieve every goal you set. Sometimes you are not committed to pay the price, sometimes the goal wasn't that important, and sometimes things change. What you want for your life while you are single will change once you have a family. What you want to achieve in your career when you are twenty-three may be different when you are thirty-three.

The process of setting goals is a journey. What is important to remember is that the effort of defining your goals and writing them down sets you in motion. That motion moves you forward, and forward momentum sometimes leads you to forks in the road that you would not have encountered otherwise. When standing at one of these forks in the road, you may find a new path that offers even greater opportunities for success and happiness.

Setting Goals Is Simple

The first, and most important, step towards getting what you want is to define it and write it down. Unfortunately, this simple step has been over-complicated by many goal setting gurus. You can find their varied methodologies on the shelves of your favorite bookstore. Please don't get me wrong, there are hundreds of books and audio programs on setting goals which offer great value.

My point is, in the span of fifteen minutes you can set five to ten key goals for the next year. In the course of an hour, day or a week you can set goals for the next three, five or ten years. Invest an hour or so a month to review, rewrite or set new goals and you will change your life. It really is this simple. Don't over-complicate it. Define it and write it down!

The Rules

There are a few basic rules you should follow when writing down your goals: *Goals Must be Specific, Goals Must be Time Bound, Goals Must be Attainable and of course, Goals Must be Written Down.* It is important to shoot for the stars and ignore the limits, but if too many of your goals are long shots you'll end up becoming frustrated. Getting regular wins helps you stay motivated and on track.

Most importantly, big goals are always achieved through a series of small, measurable steps, and these *Steps to Success* (your plan) must be defined in the same manner. Later in this chapter, I'll introduce you the *PowerPrinciples Goal Sheet*™ which is designed to help you with this process.

The Rules

Goals Must Be Specific

Goals Have Measurable Steps to Success

Goals Must be Attainable

Goals Must Be Time Bound

Goals Must Be Written Down

Goals Must Be Specific

Goals must be specific. This means exact, clear, precise, and unambiguous. For example, if you want to be successful, you will never have success until you define specifically what success means to you. It takes work to be unambiguous with your goals. Sometimes it makes sense to have someone coach you. When I help Sales Professionals define what they want and set specific goals, a typical conversation goes something like this:

Jeb: So tell me what you want.

Jill: Huh?

Jeb: What do you want out of your life?

Jill: Oh. I don't know. I guess to be happy.

Jeb: That's awesome. What does that mean, you know, to be happy?

Jill: Well, I guess I just want to be content.

Jeb: Okay. So help me out here. Tell me what it means to be content.

Jill: (Blank stare – silence)

Jeb: (Stares back – silence)

Jill: What do you mean?

Jeb: Give me an example of what content means to you.

Jill: Well for one thing it means I don't have to worry about money.

Jeb: How do you mean?

Jill: One of the things I worry about now is buying a home. I rent an apartment and I want to own my own home. To do that I need to have a down payment and I'm trying really hard to save.

Jeb: So are you saying that to feel happy and content you need to own your own home?

Jill: Yes, when you put it that way I guess you are right. I think about this all of the time and I worry about how I'm going to get the down payment I need to buy the house I want.

Jeb: OK, is there anything else?

Jill: Yes, there are other things but owning my own home is the main thing. I really want that bad.

Jeb: Excellent. May I ask a question?

Jill: Sure.

Jeb: What kind of house do you want to own?

Jill: Oh I don't know – just a house of my own.

Jeb: Jill, I'm sure you've closed your eyes and dreamed. What does this house look like when you dream?

Jill: (she smiles) Well, it is a stucco house with a natural stone façade. They are building them in a new neighborhood called Riverchase.

Jeb: That sounds awesome. Tell me more.

Jill: Well I want it to have three bedrooms and a den I can use as an office and I want a granite kitchen with stainless steel appliances.

Jeb: It sounds like you've given this some thought.

Jill: (Big smile) I guess I have. I really want this place.

Jeb: (pulls out a *PowerPrinciples Goal Sheet*™) Let's get to work on getting you that house!

Make Goals Tangible

This is how I help people define what they want. The key is helping them move from general wants to specific, tangible goals. With some practice you can learn how to frame questions like these for yourself. Specific goals are powerful motivators. When you take time to set and write down goals you naturally begin to visualize the outcome.

The Goal, "I will take my family on a vacation" is ambiguous. Goals like, "I will take my family on vacation to Disney World, the second week in July. We will stay in the Animal Kingdom Lodge and we will (*fill in the blank*), and we will (*fill in the blank*)" help you visualize your family at Disney with smiles on their faces.

Powerful imagery attaches tangibility to your goals. When you can touch, feel and see your goals you unleash powerful forces that drive and motivate you to do what it takes to reach them.

Goals Must Be Time Bound

Once you have defined exactly what you want, the next question that must be answered is *"When?"* The act of defining "when" places urgency on your actions. Urgency is critical to achieving both long-term and short-term goals. With long-term goals, urgency forces us to focus on the little steps that lead to the larger goal. With short-term goals, urgency forces action, harnessing our desire, to remove complacency and procrastination.

Defining "when" also keeps you realistic about the work you have to do to obtain your goals. If you are unrealistic about the amount of time it will take to reach your goals you may end up frustrated or dejected. Of course, there is always the chance that you push your deadlines so far out into the future that you fail to reach your full potential, and end up with less than you could have had.

I have fallen into both of these traps. Most recently, when I set my goal to write this book, I was too ambitious with the deadline. I became so frustrated when I realized I would miss my target that I quit writing. In time, I was able to get back on track, but the lost momentum was a major setback.

"When you set goals, something inside of you starts saying, 'Let's go, let's go,' and ceilings start to move up."
- Zig Ziglar

Goals Must Be Written Down

When you write down your goals, ink on paper, you tap into a powerful force. This same force is not present when you just think about your goals. It only comes into play when you write them down. I wish I had eloquent words to describe why writing down your goals is so powerful. My friend David said it best though, "It's like magic!"

I've experienced this phenomenon over and over again in my own life and observed it in the lives of others. A written goal forces action. Something inside of you begins to drive you forward. The goal you've written down constantly tugs at you, pulling and pushing you towards your destination. It is there, written in stone, and it cannot be ignored until it has been accomplished.

Risky Business

Writing down goals is risky business, which is why so few people actually do it. What's the risk? You risk failure. The fear of falling on your face keeps you from committing. Then there is the work involved. That can be risky, too. When you write down your goals, action becomes a requirement. Action is work and subconsciously we would rather rest on easy street. Stepping out of our comfort zone is scary. But, oh, how the world will open up to you once you take that step!

To overcome fear we must face fear and I want you to do that right now. *On a blank piece of paper, write down one goal you will accomplish in the next thirty days. Do not move ahead until you have applied ink to paper!*

Steps to Success

Once you've defined your specific goals and committed to a realistic time line, you'll want to develop an action plan. An excellent way to capture these *Steps to Success* in written form is to use the *PowerPrinciples Goal Sheet*™ (go to www.SalesGravy.com to download a free copy).

The PowerPrinciples Goal Sheet™ has three parts.

1. **My Goals:** *specific and attainable*
2. **My Deadline:** *time bound*
3. **My Steps to Success:** *measurable plan*

The most common and limiting mistake people make in setting goals is a failure to build a plan. In sales, the *Steps to Success* are straight forward because they are almost always defined in terms of measurable sales activities. Typically these activities include things like the number of cold calls (by phone and in person), referrals, networking events, first time visits, return visits, proposals or product demonstrations. There are also levers like the size of the deals you sell, product mix, re-orders, gross margins, etc... There are endless combinations. The trick is to develop the right plan for you, which depends on your desired outcome and industry. Be prepared to be flexible and ready to adjust as situations change and time passes.

Jill's Steps To Success

Once Jill set her goal to buy a house, we began

working on her *Steps to Success*. Jill determined that she would put a down payment of 20% on her new home. She set a deadline of one year to have her down payment saved. Based on the cost of the home and what she already had in the bank, she calculated that she would need to save an additional $725 a month. This would be a stretch.

Our next step was analyzing her current sales activity and the income resulting from that activity. From there we discussed the activities she would need to change to increase her income. After considering all of the possibilities, she came to the conclusion that she would need to add one additional sale each week at her current commission rates to make her goal.

This meant she would need to increase her telephone prospecting dials from 25 to 50 a day which would effectively double the number of opportunities in her sales funnel. That would naturally increase her first time appointments, product demonstrations, and proposals - resulting in one additional sale each week.

Of course, the additional activity would mean more work and require some behavioral changes. She would have to get up earlier and plan her cold calling lists more effectively. She would need to set aside time for planning her week on Sunday and review her plan each afternoon. Good time management would be critical.

Jill worked hard. She doubled her dials and subsequently doubled her deals. She made so much more in commissions that she got way ahead of her savings goal. After she moved in to her new house she told me that she had learned a valuable lesson: *big goals are always accomplished through a series of small, measurable steps.* I was impressed!

"Life is a series of steps. Things are done gradually. Once in a while there is a giant step, but most of the time we are taking small, seemingly insignificant steps on the stairway of life." - Ralph Ransom

The Law of Congruency

I was having a coaching conversation with Cory, a Sales Professional from Houston. I asked him about his goals and in the ensuing discussion he told me he wanted to save enough money to send his three children to college. He lamented that his parents had no money to pay for school and he didn't want his children to have to work as hard as he did to get an education. I couldn't help thinking, "What an amazing Dad!"

I asked a few more questions to get a better understanding of how much more he needed to save. He had a long way to go. Our analysis of his situation told us that if he was going to meet his savings goal he would need to start putting away an additional $600 per month. This seemed like a lot to me, but Cory, standing his ground, said he was determined to make it happen. So we pulled out a *PowerPrinciples Goal Sheet*™ and wrote down his *Steps to Success,* which included increased sales activity and some personal sacrifices.

Several months later I was back in Houston and looked Cory up to find out how he was doing with his college savings plan. Cory said he wasn't making much progress towards his goal but he was "getting things lined up" and planned to start soon. After our discussion I was convinced that Cory would never reach his college savings targets for his children because he was unwilling to pay the price it would take both in terms of increased sales activity and personal sacrifice. He was doomed to fail because no matter how badly he wished to accomplish his goal he would not take action to get it. Instead, he would take the easy road and leave his kids' college savings to hope and luck.

The Law

Cory's problem was that his goal and what he was willing to do to achieve his goal were not congruent. Congruency is an important concept in the game of goal setting. The Law of Congruency simply states that what you want and the price you are willing to pay (the actions you are willing to take) to get what you want must match.

Often, we are more than willing to set a goal but unwilling to do the work required. The price for our goal is just too high for us, and sometimes with good reason. If, for instance, you want to be a Sales Manager, which means you must sacrifice many nights away from your family and take a potential income reduction; perhaps the price is too high and you should choose a goal more congruent with your values.

Be Realistic

Wasting time on unattainable goals impedes your progress leaving you both frustrated and feeling like a failure. Your awareness that goals and actions must be congruent will lead you to become more realistic about the price it will cost you to attain your goals. A dose of reality will help you build better *Steps to Success* and shore up the self discipline you will need to be successful.

Start Now!

Define what you want and write it down. It isn't much more complicated than this. Stop reading, put this book down, and start thinking about what you want. Be honest with yourself. Don't go forward in this book until you have defined at least one goal and written it down.

When you clearly define what you want, you have great power in your hands. It is at that point when your dreams take on tangible shape and you take control of your life's design!

On the next page I want you to write down at least one goal you will accomplish in the next year. Then I want you to define your *Steps to Success*. Use the *PowerPrinciples Goal Sheet*™ as a guide, (*you can download a free copy at www.SalesGravy.com*). This exercise won't be easy, so be prepared to think. Consider how you can leverage your talents as a Sales Professional to reach this goal.

Once you define what you want and write it down, with some work, you will begin reaping the rewards you deserve from your sales career. Stop reading and start now!

PowerPrinciples Goal Sheet™				My Deadline
Year_____				
My Goals				**My Deadline**
Income Goals				
Annual:	Monthly:	Weekly:	Hourly:	
Goal				
Goal				
Goal				
Goal				

My Steps to Success

	Activity	Quantity	Frequency	Planned Result
1.				
2.				
3.				
4.				
5.				
6.				
7.				
8.				
9.				
10.				

Resources

Visit www.salesgravy.com for additional resources to help you set and reach your goals.

- Download a free *PowerPrinciples Goal Sheet*™.

- Get a **Coach** to help you.

- Join **eLife Plans**, the online goal tool.

- Subscribe to **eGravy** - the free weekly Success e-Zine.

- Subscribe to the Sales Gravy: PowerPrinciples **Podcast**

- Search the **eGravy Archives** for goal related articles.

- Browse our recommended **Reading List.**

- Schedule **Jeb** to speak to your group.

- **Contact Us** for more information on goals.

- **Leave a Testimonial** - tell us about your success.

www.salesgravy.com

POWERPRINCIPLE #2

Invest In Yourself

"Sales Professionals are the elite athletes of the business world."

The Best Habit

Debbie was so tired that she was having a hard time staying focused. We'd scheduled dinner to spend time catching up on careers, politics, and the emerging trends in sales and marketing, but instead she was explaining how hard it was to find time for the things she needed to do for herself. It was easy to see how frustrated and stressed she was. As I listened to her plight, I couldn't help thinking about the many times I had heard the same complaint from other professionals. It is so easy to burn out and it often happens to us without notice, until of course, it is too late.

Debbie is driven. She gives tirelessly to her organization, clients, and employees. She has achieved levels of success unexpected of someone her age. The problem she faced was, as she gave pieces of herself (her energy) to others, she was not scheduling time to replenish. Fortunately, she was aware that it was beginning to impact her well-being, peace of mind, and happiness. We discussed her situation and the options she had available for reading, relaxing, thinking, and exercising. She walked away from our discussion with one assignment: *she would schedule time on her calendar each day for herself and that appointment would not be broken.*

About six months later I checked in on her progress. Debbie's relaxed tone of voice told me all I needed to know. She explained how she was going to the gym or yoga classes daily and how she had almost caught up on her professional reading. I could hear her smiling on the phone as she proudly told me she had just been promoted to Senior Vice President. Despite the fact that she was given more responsibility with higher expectations, she said she had never felt better in her life.

She explained, "Learning to block out time on my calendar just for me is one of the best habits I've ever formed. It's funny how we will plan and schedule business meetings, sales calls, and client events, and then leave our most important appointment, time for investing in ourselves, to chance."

Elite Business Athletes

Sales Professionals are the elite athletes of the business world. We are the real key to business success. Without successful sales people most businesses would quickly fail. Look at it like this. If your company were a professional football team, the sales and marketing professionals would be on the field playing and everyone else would be working in support roles. Just as an NFL team counts on its players to deliver in the game, your company counts on its elite athletes (you) to deliver on the street.

Elite athletes train to keep mind, body, and spirit in pristine shape. When elite athletes take the field they are in the game to win! Like athletes, to be your best, to win on the street, you must invest in yourself through a regime of physical, intellectual and spiritual exercise.

"Life is a hard grader!"
- Cyndi Gundy, Instructor, University of Central Florida, School of Marketing

Sales Is Brutal

The work we do in sales is hard. The pressure to sell, the demand to perform is unrelenting. We must deliver results or we will be fired. In sales it is all or nothing! We have but one number: *Quota*. Miss quota and you are out. Exceed quota and you are a hero. In sales, you are not judged by what you have done, but rather what you have done today!

Sales is brutal and few can stand the pressure. We live each day with rejection. The mental and physical toll on hard-working Sales Professionals is unrelenting. Recruiters and HR professionals will attest that it is very difficult to find people who are willing to endure these hardships. Most people wouldn't last a minute in your shoes. Even for those rare and special people who thrive in the sales environment, it is easy to burn out.

Little Pieces Of You

On a typical day, elite Sales Professionals get started in the wee hours of the morning. Many have to get their families ready for the day before they can even start thinking about sales activity. You may even be a single parent juggling the responsibilities of parenthood and a full time sales job. It is hard to imagine the character and fortitude it takes for you to stay focused.

Once you get to the office, most of you start your sales day by prospecting and following up on leads. Prospecting generates many "NOs", and each no, each rejection, takes a little piece of you. Most Sales Professionals receive more rejection before 9:00 am than the average person gets in an entire year!

Then you go on appointments, you make presentations, you tour facilities, you ask questions, you gather information, you give product demonstrations and showings, you endure conversations with your customers at lunches and dinners, you give proposals and you close deals. Sometimes you hear yes! Many times you hear maybe. But because you are in sales, more often than not, you hear no, No, NO! Every no takes a little piece of you.

Finally after a day of battle on the streets you come back to the office and fight for your customers. You remove road blocks, deal with negative people and fix problems. You deal with back orders. You answer to the boss. You fight the office. You fight for contract approvals, for credit approvals, and many times for commissions or bonuses. Every problem, every roadblock takes a little piece of you.

At the end of the day you go home. You deal with your spouse, your kids, your pets, your neighbors, the bills, and a million other things. But because you are in sales your mind never stops. You think about the deals lost, the opportunities, the wins, the boss, and the roadblocks. Your energy is drained, your belief system deteriorates, and the stress takes a physical toll. In sales, the rewards are great, but if you don't put those pieces back, eventually you will burn out and you will fail!

Put Those Pieces Back!

The problem you face is that there is no one to fill you up again except you. So it is absolutely critical that you take steps to invest in yourself: *mind, body, and spirit.* You have to refill your heart and soul. Take time to focus on you. Take time to reenergize and build your positive attitude. Take care of your spirit and your mental well-being. You've got to take time everyday to read books about sales and motivation. You must make it a habit to turn off the radio while you are in your car and listen, instead, to motivational or spiritual programs. Exercise daily so that you stay in top physical condition. Eat and drink in moderation. Pay attention to what you are putting into your mouth. Get plenty of sleep.

Success in investing in yourself rests with your discipline to set time aside, written on your calendar, just for you. This appointment with yourself must be as sacred as a meeting with a top prospect, customer, your boss or your child's piano recital. When you are strong and healthy you gain the Winning Edge. You shrug off rejection. If you are knocked down you get up faster and still have the energy to fight back and win. Put those pieces back!

"Cultivation of the mind is as necessary as food to the body." - Cicero

Invest in Your Mind

Ghandi said, "We should live as if we will die tomorrow and learn as if we will live forever." I've observed that Sales Professionals who continually exercise their intellect are happier, more motivated and invariably more successful than their peers. They take advantage of every training program their company offers and are always the first people standing in line when there is an opportunity to learn something new. They invest their own money in seminars and workshops to keep their skills updated and sharp. They subscribe to weekly e-zines, trade magazines, and sales publications to stay current on the science of sales. They learn as if they will live forever and in doing so outpace their competitors. These Sales Professionals understand that by investing in the mind, they acquire the knowledge and skills required for accomplishment and success.

Read!

Everything you ever need to know about anything is contained in a book. Everything! If you want to learn something or become an expert at something all you have to do is read. Most of you want to be the very best in your profession. A key to becoming the best is to have more knowledge about the sales profession than anyone else.

There are thousands upon thousands of books and articles on the art and science of sales. I'm positive that at least some of these books sit on your bookshelf but have never been read. Do you desire to read them? Sure, but you don't. It's not easy to find time to read when you have a full time sales career, a family, friends, and all of the obligations of life. The thing is, when you don't take time for professional reading, you quickly fall behind your competitors and ultimately give away your Winning Edge.

The problem for most of us is that we look at all of those books and get overwhelmed. We think to ourselves, "How in the world will I ever get to them all? It's just too much!" Then, because we are overwhelmed, we procrastinate.

As a Sales Manager, I discovered that there was a strong correlation between reading and sales success. Usually when I had a rep who was failing, I'd also find that they were doing no professional reading. One of my Sales Professionals, Jim, had talent, skill and desire, but his pipeline wasn't in good shape. His numbers were suffering and he was losing confidence in himself.

I called Jim into my office and we discussed his predicament. Jim developed a detailed plan to get out of his slump. His plan included 15 minutes of professional reading each day before he started his phone block. The first book Jim chose to read was No Bull Selling, by Hank Trisler.

The results were off the charts. Jim won the top sales award that quarter and ended the year #1 on the team. He was subsequently promoted to Sales Manager, and then to Director of Sales. I spoke to Jim recently and he told me that he continues his reading routine today. He has become one of the leading and most knowledgeable professionals in his industry. He is viewed by his organization and the people who work for him as an expert. By reading just 15 minutes a day, Jim has read hundreds of books on sales, leadership, and business.

The secret to overcoming reading procrastination

is to break reading into small doses. Just 15 to 30 minutes of professional reading daily will have an amazing impact on your life. Pick a time of day that makes sense for your schedule, block it out on your calendar, and keep this appointment with yourself.

Do The Math

Fifteen minutes a day of professional reading adds up fast. Most people who make a commitment to this practice are shocked at how many books they go through. When I speak to groups I'll often walk through the math just to make this point. Here's how it works:

There are 52 weeks in a year. Assuming that we only do our professional reading on week days, and that we take two weeks off for vacation, we are left with 250 days for professional reading. If we multiply 250 days by 15 minutes that gives us 3,750 minutes or roughly 62.5 hours of professional reading in a year. The average business, sales or personal development book requires about three hours to read. When we do the math (62.5/ 3) we determine that over the course of a year, when you read just fifteen minutes a day, you will read approximately 21 professional books.

This is an astounding number of books. At every *PowerPrinciples* seminar, without fail, someone will yell out, "I haven't read twenty-one books in my life!" Reading just fifteen minutes a day will change your life. Over the years it will add up to a college education many times over. Get started today. Grab a piece of paper and write down five books you will commit to reading this year.

Seminars and Speakers

There are experts on sales, business, and personal development who conduct seminars or who are speaking in every city. For most of us it seems impossible to take time out of our busy schedules to attend these events. The truth is, you can't afford not to go. Some of the brightest minds in business are speaking in your city today. They are speaking to civic groups, chamber groups or conducting stand alone seminars. Smart Sales Professionals and business leaders make it a point to hear at least one speaker or attend one seminar each quarter.

Drive Time

Drive time is an excellent time to invest in your mind. The average outside Sales Professional spends between 10 and 20 hours a week in a car. Sadly, many spend that time listening to music or talk radio instead of learning by listening to a book on CD, a language program or an instructional program. I realize drive time is also spent on the phone prospecting, maintaining relationships, and closing deals. Still, at a minimum, we have at least an hour a day of downtime riding in our cars. So why not spend that time listening to something good for you? The great Zig Ziglar calls this "Automobile University." Zig maintains that by just listening to educational and personal development audio programs in your car you can gain the equivalent of a university education.

I credit the hours and hours I have had listening to educational and motivational programs in my car with much of the success I've had as a Sales Professional and Sales Leader. As a sales person, I listened to Brian Tracy's <u>Psychology of Selling</u> so many times that I went through three sets of cassette tapes. In my car I learned about setting goals, time management, the German language, and improved my attitude. I've "read" dozens of books in my car. In fact, this past summer I "read" the unabridged version of <u>Emotional Intelligence</u> while traveling in my car.

Technology has made it even easier to carry your books and motivational programs with you. With an iPOD, I can carry my entire audio library in my pocket. Now, when I'm on planes, trains and automobiles or have some downtime I can invest in my mind by simply pushing Play.

Resources

Visit www.salesgravy.com for additional resources to help you exercise your intellect.

- Subscribe to **eGravy** - the free weekly Success e-Zine.

- Subscribe to the Sales Gravy: PowerPrinciples **Podcast**.

- Search the **eGravy Archives** for articles.

- Browse our recommended **Reading List**.

- Schedule **Jeb** to speak to your group.

www.salesgravy.com

"Health is not valued until sickness comes."
- Dr. Thomas Fuller, 18th century scientist

Invest In Your Body

What would change in your life, right now, if you began eating three healthy meals a day, dropped the junk food, and began exercising just 30 minutes every day? For many of you this step forward would change your life! You would feel better, look better and have more confidence. You would gain new energy that would propel you forward towards your goals.

The Strong Body - Strong Mind Connection

Sales is a mental game and your capacity for outwitting your competition is the winning edge. Thinking requires a tremendous amount of energy, especially in the stressful, emotional, roller coaster world of sales. Your mental energy is limited by your physical energy, so becoming physically fit naturally boosts mental energy. Major studies have proven that regular exercise improves creative thinking, mental clarity, and the capacity to bounce back from the inevitable rejection in sales.

Stamina

A motto I've carried throughout my career is *"when it's time to go home, make one more call."* This means that when it's the end of the day, you are tired, and all you want to do is quit, you must will yourself to make one more call. I can tell you first hand that "one more call" has yielded some of my biggest sales. However, it's nearly impossible to garner the stamina to keep going when your body is weak and out of shape.

You can't win if you lack the endurance to stay ahead of the pack during the long race to the finish line.

Many of you work long days running from airport to airport. Others are in and out of cars in the heat, rain, and cold. Most of you spend hours on the phone with customers and prospects. I know sales people who work so hard they have new soles put on their shoes every two or three months. How can you stay ahead of the competition, and perform like an elite athlete, in this environment, if you are not in tip top shape? You need stamina in the tough world of sales. Just like an athlete you must be prepared to go the extra mile and break through the limits so that at the end of the day when your competitors pack up and go home, you make one more call.

Confidence

Prospects and customers judge you by your physical appearance. They want to do business with winners and winners look and feel confident. You know the feeling you get when you put on a new suit and look in the mirror? Your shoulders go up, your chin goes up and you instantly feel confident. When your body is in great shape that feeling is multiplied a hundred times. You exude confidence. Confidence wins deals. Confidence gets you bigger commission checks. Confidence is a defining trait of consistent winners.

Sweat 30 Minutes A Day

Being in great shape is critical for sustainable success yet, hard working Sales Professionals struggle to find time. How will you add a fitness routine to an already busy schedule? It is not as hard as you may think. The first step is to commit to 30 minutes of exercise a day. If you are really crunched for time you can even break your scheduled exercise into two 15 minute blocks.

The easiest forms of exercise are right in your own backyard. Take a walk or ride your bike when you get home at night. Supplement this with 50 sit-ups and 50 push-ups. On the weekends play sports or go for a hike. What if you walked and carried your bag on the golf course instead of riding in a cart?

I have a good friend whose motto is *"sweat 30 minutes a day, find a way."* For him, it doesn't matter what the activity is as long as it gets his heart rate up and sweat comes out of his body. There are literally hundreds of ways to build a 30-minute-a-day workout routine into your busy life. It doesn't matter what you do, it just matters that you do something that makes you sweat, for at least 30 minutes every day.

Rules For Food

Food is the central element in maintaining your health. In the hectic, driven world of sales it can be difficult to eat well. The good news, these days is that even fast food restaurants have healthy choices. With just a little discipline and planning you can easily find nutritious food on the road and you can certainly prepare healthy meals at home.

There are a couple of rules for eating that I live by. The first rule is moderation. I love food and some of the food I love is bad for me. I don't deprive myself, but I don't go overboard either. Enjoy your life and eat the things you like, but eat in moderation both in terms of what you eat and how much you eat.

One of the big problems with dieting is that dieting by its very nature violates the rule of moderation. Dieting takes us from one extreme, eating too much of the wrong foods, to the other extreme, eating too little of foods that don't satisfy us. When we get out of balance, it is more likely that we will swing back to our old habits fast and hard.

The second rule is that breakfast is mandatory. No matter what, eat something for breakfast, even if it is a cold piece of pizza. Breakfast is the most important meal of the day, it kick-starts your metabolism, energizes your attitude, and it helps you with the discipline to eat a healthy lunch.

Do The Math

Thirty minutes a day of exercise produces tremendous results. Even after we do the math you may have a hard time coming to grips with the shear number of calories you will burn. Take a look:

There are 52 weeks in a year. Assuming that we only exercise five days a week, and that we take two weeks off for vacation, we are left with 250 days for exercising. Walking briskly on a treadmill, you will conservatively burn 140 calories over 30 minutes of exercise. If we multiply 140 calories by 250 days we'll burn approximately 35,000 calories over the course of a year.

The secret to losing weight is this: *"Calories in" must be less than "Calories out."* It is as simple as that. Just eat and drink in moderation, exercise 30 minutes a day and you will lose weight and feel better about yourself. You will never need to diet again and at the same time you will stay in excellent condition.

Outlast Your Competitors

Over the years I've heard many wise people say that we never appreciate our good health until we no longer have it. Without your good health, you have little chance of leading a happy and fulfilled life. It will be difficult, if not impossible, to live your dreams and you certainly cannot be there for the people you love.

Sales is physically and mentally demanding. The stress you endure is intense and unrelenting. You must be in peak condition to deliver peak performance. Elite Sales Professionals keep their bodies in excellent shape, and in doing so outlast their competitors at every turn.

"Feed your faith and your fears will starve to death." - Unknown

Invest In Your Spirit

Spirituality is a sensitive subject that in today's business world is often taboo. There is good reason for this. We all have different sets of beliefs about our spirituality, that when challenged, can leave us feeling emotionally charged. Because spirituality is so personal and emotional, I had great difficulty writing this section of the book. I could not find words I felt would artfully convey the correlation between investing in the spirit and getting what you want out of life.

So I began interviewing successful people and eventually found that no matter the religious background, practices or beliefs, all of these successful people shared a common understanding about spirituality and its role in helping them reach their goals. At the core, this group of highly successful people, all from different backgrounds, believe that there is something or someone bigger than them working in their lives. They believe that everything in life is connected and have faith that everything happens for a reason. They believe that a higher good is looking out for them and wants abundance in their lives. They believe that the spirit requires nourishment, exercise, and constant attention.

You Are What You Believe

Investing in your spirit is, in essence, an investment in a strong belief system. Your belief system determines your attitude, perspective, and confidence. For instance, if like the successful people mentioned in the proceeding paragraph, you believe that everything happens for a reason, your perspective and attitude on

POWERPRINCIPLES: DO YOU HAVE THE WINNING EDGE?

potentially negative events will be optimistic. Instead of complaining, "Why me?", you exclaim, "How can I learn from this?"

What you believe can either attract success or send it away. Your beliefs determine how happy you will be and research shows, how long you will live. They will determine the quality of your relationships and the quality of your work. Your beliefs drive your attitude and as the respected speaker and author Keith Harrell likes to say, "Attitude is everything."

Get Connected

Helen Keller was quoted as saying, "The best and most beautiful things in the world cannot be seen or even touched." She said that these things must be "felt with the heart." I don't know how to describe the spirit, I cannot see it or touch it, but I can feel it with my heart. I can feel when my spirit is not centered, when it is empty, when it is in need of nourishment, when it is not content and when it is not connected with who I am and what I'm supposed to be doing. Other people can tell, too. Not long ago, while speaking to a good friend of mine from Dallas, he commented, "I can sense that something is not right, you don't seem happy even though you say you are."

His insight was on the mark and it revealed to me that I had not been investing regularly in my spirit. My friend took time to coach me on reconnecting spiritually and recommended a few books to read. I took his advice and felt better, almost immediately.

Your spirit is the embodiment of your beliefs and it manifests itself in your outward attitude. It is a compass that helps you navigate through the rough and windy waters of life. Your spirit requires constant attention and cannot be ignored. When your spirit is not well, you are not well, and you will lose your winning edge.

Many people I know spend just five to ten minutes in quiet meditation or prayer at the beginning of each day. During this time they contemplate their purpose in life, they open themselves up to inspiration, reflect on their dreams, and with humility consider their blessings. This quiet time helps them stay connected spiritually. The people who practice this daily ritual will tell you that without it they are not centered and focused on the day.

One Sales Manager described this connection as a relationship with a friend. He said, "Think about a friend whom you only call once a year. No matter how long you had to catch up you wouldn't be very connected. But, what if you spoke to that friend on the phone for just a few minutes every day, would you be close? Absolutely! Over time you would build a tremendous connection and bond that would be impossible to break."

He explained that it is the same with the spirit. His daily visit through prayer keeps him connected and bonded to his spiritual path.

He added, "The best advice I can give anyone is to stay focused on your spiritual connection everyday and if you are feeling off-center, stop what you are doing and dial in."

Good Karma

An investment in your spirit goes beyond meditation and prayer. I once saw a homeless man in

Miami standing at the bottom of an off ramp on I-95 holding a cardboard, handwritten sign that said *Get Good Karma Here*. I laughed when I saw the sign and handed him ten dollars. It felt good helping him out and I realized that his sign was a reminder that service to others is a great way to invest in the spirit. I thought how wonderful it would be if there were a big, bright neon sign over every opportunity to serve another person that read *Get Good Karma Here*!

One of the great truths in life, is that what you give in service to others, will come back to you ten-fold. Service to others doesn't need to be complicated. It can be something you do or something you give. It can be your tithe or working as a volunteer. Service can be helping a neighbor or giving a hand to a fellow Sales Professional who needs inspiration or guidance. It can be spending time with someone to help them get what they want out of life - helping them achieve their goals. Service strengthens and builds the spirit. It helps us maintain our humility and leaves us feeling confident and energized.

Fill Up!

There are many ways to invest in your spirit. I am crazy about motivational audio programs. I love to listen to Les Brown. When Les speaks his words lift my spirit and give it wings to soar. I know a Sales Professional who listens to her preacher's sermons on CD while she drives to see customers. She says it inspires her to serve her customers and reminds her to stay humble. Taking time to read spiritual books, your book of worship or inspirational writings helps you anchor your beliefs and build your spirit. Going to your place of worship with your family is one of the best ways to fill up.

A great teacher once said, "Just as a candle cannot burn without fire, man cannot live without a spiritual life." Everyone is different and there is no right or wrong way. Find the best path for you, and start this minute, in your own way, to invest in your spirit.

A Delicate Balance

I think we all know, instinctively, that there is a connection between the mind, body, and spirit. This delicate balance is the difference between happiness and suffering. It is the line that separates real success and ultimate failure. A strong body begets a strong mind and a strong mind is the foundation for a strong spirit; but, when our spirit is weak so too are our mind and body. The discipline to invest in our physical well-being, expand our intellect, and strengthen our belief system is perhaps the most difficult of all human endeavors.

I have an auto-pilot on my boat, Sea Monkey. The auto-pilot is tied to a compass and GPS. It is designed to make cruising over long stretches of open water easier and to ensure that the most efficient course is maintained. Out on the ocean, though, there are waves, currents, and wind. These outside forces are always working together to push the Sea Monkey off course and the auto-pilot is constantly adjusting for these outside influences to maintain our heading. On a typical trip we are off course a degree or two here and there at least 80% of the time. However, because the auto-pilot is getting input from the compass and GPS, the boat maintains its course and we arrive at our destination safe and sound. If, however, the auto-pilot lost contact with these directional tools, unchecked, the results would be disastrous.

We've all experienced euphoria when our mind, body, and spirit are balanced and connected just as we have each suffered pain when these powerful connections come unglued. As an elite athlete of the business world you will be in a constant struggle to maintain this powerful equilibrium. Just like the auto-pilot on a boat, most of the time, you will be out of balance a few degrees here and there. You must make constant adjustments, always checking your bearings, to maintain your course, and arrive safely at your destination.

Stay Connected To Your Relationships

In his best selling book, <u>Never Eat Alone</u>, Keith Ferrazzi explores the impact and power relationships have on our success and happiness. He reminds his readers that scientific research has proven again and again that people who maintain strong, connected, relationships are happier, more content, healthier, and live longer lives. The human soul yearns for company. It has an innate need to interact with others. This desire is heightened in Sales Professionals, who by their very nature, have a unique talent for connecting with others. Besides companionship, your friends and family act as a compass and will quickly let you know when you are off course. They also fill your spirit and support your belief system.

Unfortunately, as Keith Ferrazzi notes, many people jettison their relationships when they are working to restore balance in their lives. In their quest to find more time for what they perceive are the most important tasks, they spend less time with the people they care about most. In doing so they lose their compass and deplete their soul of the nourishment it gets from positive, personal relationships.

The lesson Keith teaches is that we feed our spirit by staying connected. Balance is about having more people in our lives not less.

The Sound Of Silence

William Penn wrote, "True silence is the rest of the mind; it is to the spirit what sleep is to the body, nourishment and refreshment." I passionately believe that we must schedule, on our calendars, at least thirty minutes each week just to think. No distractions, no music, no TV, no laptop, no Blackberry, just you and your thoughts, alone. Taking time to just think is powerful. It slows you down, helps you relax and frequently generates incredible ideas and inspiration. Silence provides you with the capacity to contemplate where you are and where you are going.

The first time you attempt to quietly think will not be easy. In the 21st century, we are not accustomed to silence. We are multitaskers! We have so many things going on at once and so much noise in our lives that it has become almost impossible to think. It will take time to build a habit of quiet contemplation and may take a few months before it becomes natural for you.

Give it a try today. Sit down in a quiet place, breathe slowly and listen closely to your inner voice. Just like a GPS it always knows where you are and will tell you when you are on the wrong path or when you are on the right path. Unfortunately, on most days, through all of the noise in our lives, we either can't hear our inner voice or choose to ignore what it is saying. Take time to think and listen. Once you form this habit and make it a weekly ritual you will tap into amazing power which will deliver peace of mind, inspiration, and balance.

You Are The Most Important Person In Your Life!

"If the cabin loses pressure", the Flight Attendant explains over the airplane PA, "an oxygen mask may drop from the ceiling. Put your oxygen mask on first, before assisting others." If you travel, you've heard this speech a hundred times. The message is simple. Take care of yourself first so that you can help others. Most of us have a difficult time coming to grips with this concept in our own lives.

On the surface it seems counter-intuitive that we have to take care of ourselves first. We are taught from an early age to put the needs of others first. However, consider this. If you give and give, without first taking care of yourself, you head down a path towards physical and mental disaster.

I'm not saying that in learning to view yourself as the most important person in your life that you should become the self-serving center of your own universe. You don't need to sacrifice your priorities or relationships to invest in yourself. However, you can not be of service to anyone if you are not taking care of you.

Enter time on your calendar for you. Keep that appointment! No one else can exercise for you, no one else can eat a healthy diet for you, no one else can learn for you, and no one else can be spiritual for you. Your happiness, success and well-being depend on your investment in you. Successful Sales Professionals know this *PowerPrinciple* well. Invest in yourself because no one else will or can.

POWERPRINCIPLE #3

A Little Bit Every Day

> *"Tim had failed at the daily disciplines of eating and exercising for far too long and even I had to admit that his goals were daunting."*

Daily Disciplines

A few years ago I received a call from a Sales Manager who was living in Seattle. His name was Tim and he sounded frantic on the phone. His latest trip to see his doctor had left him in a state of shock. Over the years, as Tim built a successful career, he'd paid little attention to his health. His physician had just confronted him with the price he was paying. Tim was overweight, his cholesterol and blood pressure were too high, and he was at serious risk of a heart attack. He was devastated.

We discussed his options and the changes he would have to make to improve his health. I could tell from his tone of voice that the enormity of the task ahead was overwhelming. Tim had failed at the daily disciplines of eating and exercising for far too long and even I had to admit that his goals were daunting. The only possible path to success would be breaking his goals into small, daily action steps.

Setting Goals

Using a *PowerPrinciples Goal Sheet*™, we first wrote down his weight, blood pressure and cholesterol goals. Next, to create urgency, we established deadlines for meeting his targets. Finally, we defined his *Steps to Success*: when, what and how much he would exercise and eat; books he would read; and interim success measures.

Fortunately for Tim, the desire to stay alive is one of life's most powerful motivators. He was determined to reach his goals. He also had people close to him with skin in the game. His family, who loved him as a father and husband, counted on him as a provider. His sales team and company depended on him too. Tim is a brilliant Sales Manager and respected leader. Without him his team would have lost power and momentum. So Tim got to work, a little bit every day, and we all cheered him on.

Little Victories

It took time. At first Tim would walk around his block each morning before heading off to his office. He started parking in the back of parking lots - walking greater distances to stores and appointments. He took the stairs instead of the elevator. At first he struggled with healthy eating. However, he soon found that if every evening he packed healthy snacks for the next day, he gained the discipline to eat better meals. It wasn't long before he started seeing results. As he reached his interim goals, the small victories gave way to big wins, which motivated Tim to work even harder. Soon he was running, then he added biking and weight training. His daily disciplines developed into habits. He lost weight and his health improved.

Big Lessons

Tim called me about six months later to announce that he had entered a 5K race. Soon he was competing regularly. It took a year, but Tim's good health returned and he accomplished his goals. He also did something that I am still in awe of today. Eighteen months after sitting down with me to build his *PowerPrinciples Goal Sheet*™, Tim ran a marathon. Tim learned a valuable and important lesson from his experience. Big accomplishments are the result of the discipline to do the little things, a little bit, every day.

"Procrastination is the grave in which opportunity is buried." - Unknown

A Big Pile of Should-a-Dones

It sounds easy doesn't it? I bet you are already thinking, "A little bit every day? I can do that!"

Be careful, don't let the simplicity of this *PowerPrinciple* fool you. Consider for a moment all of the important tasks and goals in your life that have piled up around you. Look inside yourself and be truthful. What if you had not procrastinated? What would be different in your life? Where would you be now?

A Riddle

You've no doubt heard the riddle, "What is the best way to eat an elephant?" the answer, of course, is, "One bite at a time." This makes sense! It is impossible to accomplish large tasks all at once. Yet, too often, we try to eat the elephants in our lives all in one bite, which results in stress, frustration and ultimately failure.

So, if it makes sense and seems so simple why is this such a hard principle to apply? The answer: because it takes loads of self-discipline, and self-discipline is among the most rare and coveted of all human traits. Conversely, procrastination is among the most common and is an ugly disease that plagues the human race. No one is immune.

I ought to know because I have a Ph.D. in procrastination - a bona fide expert. One year I bought a book called, How to Stop Procrastinating (my New Year's resolution). That book sat unread on my bedside table for three years until I finally sold it at a garage sale. Nuts! I was in my early twenties at the time and had yet to learn the hard lesson about the discipline of doing a little bit every day.

The Price We Pay

You see, it is just in our nature as humans to procrastinate. It's easy to say, "Oh I'm tired, I'll exercise tomorrow." It's easy to say, "I'll start my diet tomorrow, I'll quit smoking after this pack, I'll make up today's prospecting on Friday, I'll start reading that book next week!" It's in our nature to fool ourselves with these promises.

But there is no reward for procrastination. To be successful at getting what you want you must have the self-discipline to do a little bit of the work towards your goal every day. You can't wait until the end of the year or even the end of the month to prospect. You have to prospect every day. If you try to do all of your prospecting for the month in one day you will fail. There is just no way to get it done. The best way to get referrals is to ask for them every day. You can't wake up once a year and declare, "This is referral day" and get all of your referrals. And so it goes for all sales activities.

Procrastinating is easy, but the cost is great. Many people don't understand the price they have paid until they wake up one day and realize that their dreams have passed them by. Instead of success, they ended up with a big pile of "should-a-dones," regrets, and failures.

Stop The Madness!

Every failure in my life has been a direct result of a collapse in my self-discipline to do the little things every day! To add insult to injury, these failures were too often accented by an embarrassing crescendo of hurried and wasted activity trying to catch-up and do it all at one time. Impossible! The failure to do the little things every day will cripple your efforts to achieve your goals. Lack of discipline will slowly but surely tug at your success and will eventually steal it away.

Desire

If it is in our nature as humans to procrastinate, how do we break the cycle and stop the madness?

The secret is harnessing your desire and your motivation so that the most important things are attended to every day. It is easier to find the self-discipline to do the hard work required each day when that work is tied to a goal or a dream. For example, if you desire more than anything to go on your company's elite sales trip, you will find the will to wake up early every morning and hit the streets.

Writing down your goals helps you harness your desire. Desire creates a spark that leads to action. Action is motion. Motion creates momentum. Momentum moves you forward towards your goals and is deadly to procrastination. Momentum, fueled by motivation, requires that you do a little bit every day to continue moving forward. Motivation trumps procrastination. It beats it into the ground!

"Desire is the mother of activity."
- Brian Stanton, Director of Sales

Success Happens a Little Bit Every day

The key to being healthy, to being happy, to great relationships and to success, is accomplishing a little bit every day.

Exercising 30 minutes a day will build endurance, strength, mental well-being, and extend your life. Reading 15 minutes a day will give you the knowledge to outwit your competitors. Investing a little bit of time, every day, with the people you love builds strong, connected and enduring relationships that will enrich your life. Just listening to a motivational audio program for a few minutes every day while you are on the way to or from your office will help you build and maintain a winning attitude.

Elite Sales Professionals understand the power of self-discipline and know that the small steps add up to huge gains in the long-term. They know that one of the great secrets of living a great life is winning a little bit every day.

Get a Coach

"He was a great coach because he cared enough about me to invest his time and effort to make sure that I walked away a winner."

Fretting and Sweating

I can't remember how many messages I'd left for Sam, but I do remember that it had taken six solid months of phone calls and letters to get an appointment. Sam was the purchasing manager for a major food processing and distribution company. Getting an appointment was critical because the contract Sam had with my competitor was expiring and the buying window was open. It was the biggest account I'd ever worked on. Closing this sale would put me on top of the sales rankings which was a place I longed to be. The day I finally got Sam on the phone, he ribbed me about all of the messages I'd left and the letters I'd sent, but was laughing when he agreed to a face to face appointment. He said, "Anyone as persistent as you deserves thirty minutes of my time."

I met Sam two days later. He had a small office with lots of papers piled up on his desk. He was hurried and seemed very busy. I opened the call with my standard thirty-second commercial and then asked some basic questions. Sam politely gave an overview of his account and told me that he was very unhappy with my competitor. I asked him about the problems and he provided some examples, but we were constantly interrupted by people walking in and the telephone ringing. Sam had allotted thirty minutes for our meeting and our time was quickly running out.

Finally Sam said, "Jeb, look, I'm really busy today. How soon do you think you will have a proposal ready?"

I responded that it would take about a week, but first I would like to talk to some of the department heads to gain a better understanding of his needs.

He stood up and started walking towards the

door. He was talking faster now and looking at his watch, "Don't worry about talking to anyone else. We are ending our relationship with your competitor and we are ready to move forward. I want to make a decision next week."

Bingo! I quickly set an appointment to bring back a proposal the next week. As I walked to the parking lot I was elated. It looked like this account was mine and I was already calculating my commission.

Stop The Presses

I rushed back to the office and canceled all of my appointments for the next week. This account was so big that it would make my year and there was no way I was going to let it slip away. I frantically called my Sales Manager to tell him about the meeting. "Bob, you are not going to believe it, these guys are going to make a change and I really hit it off with the buyer. He says he is going to make a decision next week, so I've got a lot of work to do to get ready!" Bob wasn't as enthusiastic about my prospect for a quick close and advised me to stay focused on my other accounts too. I was not planning on taking any chances so I ignored his advice.

For a week I fretted and sweated and wasted a lot of time in my excitement. I put together a beautiful PowerPoint presentation with my best slides and graphics. It was killer: great transitions, sound, and even a video. I assembled product samples and gathered my best food industry references. My pricing was very competitive and I was sure it would get Sam's attention. I practiced and practiced my presentation. For a week, I prepared and finally, I was ready.

The Big Day

The morning of my presentation to Sam I put on my best suit and tie. It was a perfect, crisp fall morning - a great day for closing the biggest account of my career. I looked in the mirror before leaving my house and said the words, "I'm an awesome salesman, this deal is mine!" Then walked confidently to my car prepared for the best day of my young sales career.

I'd asked Bob to join me for the presentation and was nervous as we sat in the lobby waiting for Sam to come get us. It was the normal case of butterflies I always felt right before a big presentation. Sam finally met us in the lobby, and with the same hurried demeanor he'd shown at our last meeting, ushered us into a conference room. Then nervously looking at his watch, said he'd be right back and left us sitting there alone.

Bob was quiet as I set up my computer to run the slide show. I tried to focus and walk though the presentation again in my head. I kept repeating positive affirmations to myself. With this deal I'd be the hero of the sales team and I was already picturing Bob giving me a big high-five in the parking lot!

A few minutes later Sam walked into the conference room followed by an older gentleman who he introduced to us as Ken, the owner of the company. I couldn't believe it. We were important enough to rate a meeting with the owner! This was looking good. Without hesitation I handed them a copy of the proposal and began the presentation.

After about five minutes, I noticed, out of the corner of my eye, that Bob was squirming in his seat. I was immediately distracted and got a sinking feeling in my gut that I had said or done something wrong. I shrugged it off and kept going. But then suddenly and loudly Bob said, "Jeb stop!"

My face flushed red with heat, my knees buckled and I thought, "Not now Bob!"

Before I could respond Bob looked across the table and said "Ken, I'm sensing that you aren't exactly impressed by our presentation."

That was when I noticed that Ken was sitting back in his chair with his arms crossed. The lines and expression on his face said it all. Then the unthinkable happened and my presentation turned into a train wreck.

Train Wreck

Ken looked directly at Bob and said, "You're damn right I'm not impressed. This is the same s@#& all of you guys bring in here. We've changed vendors four times in the last ten years and it's always for the same reasons. I just don't understand why you guys can't get it right. You know what else, this is the third presentation I've seen this week and it looks exactly like the other ones. I'm beginning to wonder if, to save money, you and your competitors have all hired the same marketing company."

Ken was pounding on the table, "I've heard the same promises over and over again. But you know what, last week your competitor shut down our line! Do you know what happens when our line gets shut down? We go out of business! We had to send every one of our employees home last Friday. That can't ever happen again! So, I'm sorry to tell you this, but I don't believe you and I don't believe your promises. You guys are all the same and I am sick and tired of listening to this!"

I was stunned. My dream of the parking lot high-five had turned into a nightmare. I had the urge to run away as fast as I could and never be seen again. I was so embarrassed it hurt.

Great Moments In Sales History

The next few moments were a blur, but I'm convinced today that I witnessed one of the greatest moments in sales history.

All six-foot-three of Bob stood up, reached over to Ken, and grabbed the proposal off of the table. Then Bob turned around and with every ounce of energy he could muster, slammed the proposal package on the floor. The sound thundered throughout the room. I looked over at Sam and his eyes were as big around as dinner plates. Then there was dead silence. I wanted to crawl under the table and disappear.

Bob slowly turned back towards Ken allowing the shock to sink in. After a moment had passed he leaned forward, looked Ken square in the eyes and said, "You're right, we are all the same, but we don't have to be."

Bob was in the zone. With all of the drama of an actor in a play, he slipped off his jacket, unbuttoned his cuffs and rolled up his sleeves. He looked at Ken and then over at Sam and matter-of-factly said, "Let's get to work. Ken, we are starting over. Tell me something, if you could design the perfect program for your company what would it look like?"

At that point Ken leaned in, his demeanor completely changed. He was all business, but there was a smile on his face as he opened up and told us exactly what he wanted. I scribbled notes as fast as I could while Bob asked follow-up questions.

When all of the questions were exhausted, Bob asked, "Is this what I hear you saying?" Then he summarized in detail the program Ken had described. Ken, smiled and nodded yes.

At that point, as I would later come to understand, Bob closed the deal. He sat back in his chair, placed his hands in his lap and asked, "If we can do this do we have a deal?"

"Absolutely", Ken replied.

Bob responded, "Okay, first we need to take a closer look at what you are doing now. Can we take a tour of your facility and meet with some of your department heads? We'll also want to look at your current inventory levels, invoices and get an understanding of how your line works."

Three hours later we had all the information needed to develop a solution to Ken's problems. We promised to be back in a week with a new proposal.

Ken shook Bob's hand and thanked him for taking time to listen to him. His final words to us were, "I'm counting on you boys."

The Lesson

Embarrassed and deflated I limped to the parking lot. As soon as we were out of ear shot Bob started issuing a laundry list of orders. I took notes. He very confidently told me that we were going to close the deal, but we had a lot of work to do first.

Then I got what I knew was coming. He asked the question, "Jeb, what did you learn today?" I just sat in silence for a moment and then spit out, "I learned that you know how to embarrass me." He grinned. I was mad and all of my anger and embarrassment poured out.

Bob was still grinning when he said, "Are you done?" Then calmly and in a relaxed tone of voice he started coaching me. "Here is what you need to make sure you learn. You screwed up because you were not working with the right person. Sam didn't have the authority to sign the check, he told you he did but he didn't. Then, instead of following our sales process you jumped over several steps and just put together a boiler plate proposal. It looked pretty, but it was ineffective because you didn't have enough information to bring them a real solution to their problems. You believed that just because Sam was unhappy with our competitor you would ink this deal."

Bob's voice was calm and his pace relaxed, "The one thing you do have going for you is that they are in the buying window. You did a great job of uncovering this opportunity and I admire your persistence in getting us in the door. We wouldn't be in the position to win this account if not for that."

"You are very lucky that Ken came to the meeting or you would have lost the sale and never known why. Over the past few hours we've had a chance to get to know Ken and his business better. You could see his body language change as he began to trust us. He likes us now and we must be absolutely perfect from here on out so that we don't lose his trust. Jeb, you need to remember that there are certain rules in sales that you cannot short cut or violate. You have learned a valuable lesson today. If you take this lesson to heart you will have sales success beyond your imagination."

Bob guided my efforts as I worked hard over the next week to develop a custom plan for Ken. We even called Ken and the Director of Purchasing and reviewed our ideas with them just to make sure we were on the same page. Bob worked with me every step of the way and continued to reinforce the lesson he was trying to teach me. He never dwelled on my mistakes and instead focused on applying the lessons to other opportunities in my sales funnel.

A week later we were once again waiting in Sam's conference room and for the first time I was experiencing something I'd never felt before: confidence. The butterflies were gone. We had done everything right this time, and I was confident we would win because we had a real plan. We presented Ken with a blueprint for a custom service program and showed him exactly how our plan would solve his problems. We also introduced a 40% pricing premium over what he was paying our competitor. Ken was true to his word though. He wanted solutions and the extra cost for our service was more than out weighed by our guarantee that his line would never be shut down. Ken was thrilled and he signed the contract right on the spot.

Two months later he sent us a letter. In his letter he said that for the first time in ten years he was happy with his service and he realized that not all companies are the same.

The Coach

This is a long story but it illustrates the power of having a great coach. I learned more about selling from that experience than from all of the classes I'd attended and all of the books I had read. Bob taught me virtually everything I know about sales. Under his watchful eye and at times strong hand, I transformed from amateur

"I absolutely believe that people, unless coached, never reach their maximum capability." - Bob Nardelli, former CEO, Home Depot

to professional.

Bob was insightful and knew how to reach deep inside of me. His unique method of teaching through examples, stories and modeling made an impact. He gave me room to learn and to question his wisdom, even when he knew I was wrong. Bob would allow me to sink, but he would never let me drown, and afterwards he would invest his time to make sure that I learned the lesson.

Everybody Needs A Coach

Shortly after I began work on <u>PowerPrinciples</u> I had an opportunity to attend the Masters golf tournament. As I walked past the clubhouse on my way to the practice tees I ran into Nick, a friend and a talented Sales Leader. Nick decided to join me and as we sat in the bleachers at the practice range, I explained that I was researching coaching for my new book. Nick chuckled and then pointed out that every one of the golfers had their own personal coach. We watched with great interest as the most talented golfers in the world listened to the instructions of their coaches. We were curious why elite professional golfers would even need coaches. The answer was obvious! There are millions of dollars at stake on the PGA Tour and tournaments are usually won by just one or two strokes. Having the right coach is often the Winning Edge.

Continuing my research on coaches, I interviewed successful people from every walk of life. Each credited their success to coaches who had helped them grow and develop. Intrigued, I contemplated the impact coaches like Bob have had on my success and the richness they've brought to my life. After months of research the facts were clear, everybody needs a coach.

The challenge we face though, is that there are plenty of people who are excellent teachers, leaders and managers. They instill knowledge and get us to work hard. True coaches, however, know how to go beyond teaching and get inside of us to motivate us to change, improve and win.

So how will you know a good coach from a poor coach? When you find a great coach how will you get them to help you?

Attract A Coach

Most of my working life has been dedicated to coaching Sales Professionals and Sales Leaders. Without doubt, the most rewarding moment for me is when a person I'm coaching has a powerful realization and suddenly gains insight on how to achieve a goal.

It isn't hard to attract me as a coach. You have to be willing to learn, listen, work hard, and make progress. Progress is the key. If I don't see you putting what you learn into practice, then coaching you loses its joy. My reward is celebrating your wins, no matter how small. If someone is resisting, defensive, or is not committed, I quickly invest my time and energy elsewhere.

When a professional golfer needs help they hire the best coach money can buy. We have the same opportunity. I've hired coaches myself and most of them have been brilliant. Most coaches are free of charge though. Many of my best coaches were my managers, some were friends, peers or people I connected with through associations, conventions, or while traveling. I'm positive, that at this very moment, there are coaches in your life but they are just not coaching you.

The secret to attracting a great coach is to be

coachable. Coaches love to coach. Their fulfillment comes from seeing you succeed. If you are not coachable, great coaches will move on to those who are. This is true even with a hired coach. I have a friend who coaches CEOs and other top executives. She earns huge sums of money to do this. She is an amazing coach and is deeply passionate about her work. However, she will walk away from people who are unwilling to be coached. The money doesn't matter to her, the coaching does.

Five Keys

I have always believed that if you are open to coaching, the right coach will come into you life, for the right reason, at the right time. There are five keys to attracting a coach:

Ask For Help: This is the first and most important step. Put away your pride, open up and ask for help.

Listen: Open your ears and your heart. Check your ego and put defensiveness aside. You must be ready to stretch.

Trust: You must have complete trust in your coach with the understanding that they are working for your best interest and can see things about you that you cannot see or will not admit.

Take Action: You must be willing to follow through on agreed upon action steps. You must be willing to do the hard work to make progress. If you are unwilling

"We must be small enough, humble enough, to always be beginners..."
- Julia Cameron, Author

or unable to complete a task then say so up front. There is nothing more frustrating for a coach than a coachee who fails to follow through.

Be Accountable: You, and only you, are responsible and accountable for your actions, goals, failures, and success. You must be willing to accept complete personal accountability for the outcome of any coaching relationship.

Moving On

Coaches help you address specific business situations, personal development, professional growth, relationship issues, goals, and life or career transitions. They examine the situation, help you discover your obstacles and challenge you to choose a course of action that will lead you to your goal.

Most coaching relationships naturally outlive their usefulness after a couple of years or so. You will eventually move on. You will graduate. Sometimes you move on because you achieved your goal or because your coach has taken you as far as they can and you need to find someone different to help you move to the next level. Several of my former coaches are great friends but they no longer have the capacity to coach me. My talents, skills, career, and life have evolved to new levels. You can count on the fact that over time things will change and you must be prepared to move on.

The Anatomy of a Great Coach

Identifying and attracting the right kind of coach is critical to getting the most out of a coaching relationship. Great coaches come from all backgrounds. They have different personality types and styles. I've known coaches who were quiet and gentle, and others who could not be ignored in a crowd.

Despite style differences great coaches share a number of core characteristics that define their ability to coach and influence other people. I have no doubt, after reading this section, you'll instantly be able to identify people in your life who have some or all of these characteristics.

Hard Lessons

The best coaching comes from someone who knows the game from the inside, who has been in the arena, who's fought the battles. They know how and when to push you beyond your self-imposed limits and sometimes they use hard lessons to teach you. A very successful Sales Professional told me a story about one of her past coaches. She said, "This guy was hard on me!"

She described how she spent a week working on the biggest proposal of her career. A few days before the big presentation she proudly showed him her work.

"This guy quietly turned the pages and then looked up at me and said: 'This is crap, you are going to have to do it again.'

"I couldn't believe it. I had worked hard and all I wanted was his approval. I was proud of my work and I was expecting a completely different response, anything other than 'this is crap.' I was so mad, I thought at that moment I was going to kill him!"

"But then, he started showing me where I had made mistakes. He helped me understand that my written proposals have to speak for me when I'm not there to speak for myself. He showed me where my recommendations were not tying back to my customer's needs."

"Then, instead of dumping on me and leaving me to fend for myself, he helped me put together a new proposal. He focused his complete attention on teaching me, yet was unyielding in his demand that I do it right."

"I learned so much from that experience. The most important thing that I learned is that in large complex sales you have to do everything perfect - even when you are tired. There is no room for error and it is almost always the individual who is willing to go the extra mile and avoid short cuts who wins the deal."

"At the time, I hated him for pushing me so hard, but I've never repeated those mistakes, and I've made a ton of money because of that lesson. He was a great coach because he cared enough about me to invest his time and effort to make sure that I walked away a winner."

There is a line in the movie *"Hoosiers"* where coach Norman Dale, says, "My practices aren't designed for your enjoyment." Good coaches feel this way. They don't spend time with you for your enjoyment. They are there to help you because they want you to be your best.

Shine A Light

A good coach will show you who you can be rather than what you are. A good friend once explained, "Most of us have been on the path to our dreams our entire life but just didn't know it. Great coaches shine a light on that path and show you how every experience you've had has moved you closer to your dreams."

Coaches are cheerleaders, advisers, motivators, sounding boards, a foot in the rear, and sometimes therapists. The best coaches will push you, frustrate you, but will never give up on you, even if sometimes, you give up on yourself. They have the courage to deal with you truthfully, in a direct and non-judgmental way, and they will stick with you on your journey, teaching, motivating, and encouraging you to win.

Key Characteristics

I've learned from experience that the best coaches focus more on you and what you want to accomplish, than on the job. They act as a human mirror showing you an outside, unbiased perspective of your behavior and actions. Most importantly, coaches ask powerful questions that shake you out of your comfort zone and challenge you to dream.

Through my research and interviews I've identified seven key characteristics to look for in coaches.

Seven Characteristics of Great Coaches

Passionate: They are passionate about growing people and they have a willingness to believe in the potential for greatness in all people. They are motivational, and they love life.

Optimistic: They are optimistic risk takers who are willing to move out of their own comfort zones to help you. They are willing to say, "I don't know," and explore where and how to learn what is needed to help you move towards your personal and professional goals.

Visionary: They are visionaries who can keep sight of the big picture even while they are deep in the details. They have a global view of the world around them.

Confident: They exude confidence, even when unsure and are resilient when life knocks them down.

Authentic: They are authentic and genuine and will relate to you on your level. They have high integrity. They will always put you first and will never compromise your relationship for their own gain.

Studious: They seek knowledge and work on their own personal development. They live to learn and teach but they clearly understand the distinction and balance between knowing and doing.

Empathic: They are great listeners who hear with their ears, eyes, and heart. They have a unique ability to empathize and step into your shoes. However, they will not allow you to live in the past. Their focus is on developing the future.

"All I know is I don't want to stop coaching."
- Bear Bryant

A Great Coach Will Change Your Life

There is a powerful scene in the movie *"Remember the Titans"* when Coach Boone says to his team: "We will be perfect in every aspect. You drop a pass, you run a mile. You miss a blocking assignment, you run a mile. You fumble the football and I will break my foot off in your John Brown hind parts and then you will run a mile. Perfection. Let's get to work." In this moment, you can feel the passion he has for his players and see that it goes beyond the football field. He wants them to be their best and he is willing to invest his time, effort and emotion, no matter what the cost, to help them become winners.

As a Sales Professional I had the talent and desire to be successful, but Bob, through his efforts, developed my skills and built a foundation on my talent. His patient teaching, pushing, prodding, encouragement, and occasional foot in my "John Brown hind parts" was the real key to my success.

The hard work of attracting coaches into your life, never ends. All successful people whether at work, life or sport have a coach standing in their corner. Coaches see what you cannot. Coaches tell you things about you that you are unwilling or unable to say to yourself. Coaches help you hone your natural God-given talents. Coaches invest themselves in your success. Great coaches change your life. If you are looking for the Winning Edge that will accelerate you towards your goals and dreams, get a coach.

Take Action

> *I wanted to shout out to the world: "You have the power inside you right now! Do something, take action, move forward!"*

You Have Power

It was a Thursday afternoon and I'd just returned from a long business trip. I was worn out and was not looking forward to going through the big stack of mail on my desk. But, it was a chore that required my attention so I grabbed a bottle of water out of the fridge and went to work. As I unenthusiastically thumbed through the bills and junk mail, I came across a small handwritten envelope addressed to me. In this day and age of email and text messaging, handwritten notes are rare and appreciated. So I stopped what I was doing and opened it. Inside was a small, white, folded note card. With anticipation I opened the card. On the inside the sender had pasted a picture of a beautiful house. Then my attention shifted to the inscription below. It read:

Dear Jeb,

Enclosed is a picture of the house my husband and I are moving into next month. Last year I saw you speak and you told us to write down five goals. Buying a house was my #1 goal. I just wanted you to see what setting goals and a great sales job have done for me. Thank you for everything!

Summer

I don't know what it was about this particular note that moved me. Maybe it was the picture of the house, her sincerity, or receiving such a heart felt note at the end of a long week. But this little card lifted my spirits and filled me with energy. I carried it around for several weeks and read it every time I needed a boost. I kept looking at it over and over again until finally deciding that I was going to track down Summer to say thank you for her kind message.

When I found her, she was in her office on the phone with a prospect. I think I surprised her because it took her a few minutes to calm down before she could speak.

Finally she gave me a big hug and said, "I can't believe you're here."

I had the note she had written in my hand and spent the next few minutes explaining how it had touched me and thanking her for taking time to tell me about her success.

Summer explained, "At that conference, when you told us to write down our goals I was skeptical. At first I didn't want to do it. But you were up on that stage and kept repeating that we had the power to make our dreams come true if we just *took action*. You convinced me!"

"Once I took that first step and put my goals on paper I couldn't believe how things just came together. I achieved every single one of my goals this year. Working hard at this sales job has really paid off. A month ago we were living in a small condo and last week we moved into a 3,100 square foot house."

She was beaming! "I've already set five new goals. I'm prospecting like crazy and I'm going to have an even bigger year than last year. I tell everyone who will listen to me about the PowerPrinciples."

I was moved. She got it! She understood the power of defining her path and taking action. I wanted to shout out to the world: "You can all be just like Summer. You have the power inside you right now! Do something, take action, move forward!"

"Don't judge each day by the harvest you reap but by the seeds you plant."
- Robert Louis Stevenson

Blind Squirrels

The power we have to take control of our own destiny is easy to forget in a society that consistently glorifies the lucky break. Hard work and dedication are often swept to the dark corners of news rooms in favor of headlines that read: *"Man wins $250,000,000 Lottery!"*

We exalt the lucky break in conversations as we talk in awe of someone who just inherited a fortune or received a big insurance settlement. Sometimes people are rewarded for doing nothing, and we romanticize these rare, lucky breaks because it helps us justify away the burden of hard work. We like to fantasize that if we just wait long enough our good luck will arrive, too. I see examples of this mindset while observing Sales Professionals putting all of their hopes into one "Hail Mary" account believing that they will somehow be rewarded even though they put no real effort into the selling process. Selling this way is no better than playing the lottery.

Reality Check

Here's a reality check, if you fail to take action, life will forget about you! There are millions of people who waste their lives waiting for their one big break. You've got a better chance of getting struck by lightning than winning the lottery. If you spend your days waiting for the slight chance that you will succeed without hard work, I can without hesitation, guarantee that you will never get what you want.

I have a very good friend who, when some poor soul gets lucky, is fond of saying, "Even a blind squirrel sometimes finds a nut." That may be true, but I've got news for you, being a blind squirrel stinks. Blind squirrels go through life hungry, bumping into trees and rocks, hoping to find a morsel here or there. Blind squirrels sometimes get lucky, but pay for that luck with a lifetime of misery and failure. Where do you stand?

- *Will you do the hard work required for success?*

- *Will you clearly define what you want and write it down?*

- *Will you invest in yourself, mind, body, and spirit?*

- *Do you have the self-discipline to do a little bit of the work every day?*

- *Will you open yourself up to coaching?*

- *Will you take action today to move your life forward?*

Or, like the blind squirrel, will you leave your success to chance?

You Reap What You Sow

The Law of Sowing and Reaping has been written about in proverbs, parables, and books dating back thousands of years. The great works of every major religion recognize and lionize the law of sowing and reaping.

To better understand this law, think of your life in the same way a farmer considers his fields. In the winter the farmer looks out over his empty fields and plans his crop. He decides what he wants to grow, how much he will grow, and when he will harvest. But what happens if, on planting day, he procrastinates, sleeps in late, or rests beneath a shady tree and fails to sow the seeds? Exactly, no crops, no food for his family, nothing to sell at the market! He can have the best laid plan, but no action results in no crops.

Farmers clearly understand the Law of Sowing and Reaping because any failure on their part to heed this law leads to disaster. How about you? How does the Law of Sowing and Reaping impact you as a Sales Professional? How does it impact your ability to get what you want out of your career and life?

Do To Get

Success is paid for in advance - you only get after you do. Life rewards nothing less. The first *PowerPrinciple* states that you can't get what you want unless you know what you want. But, if you don't take action to decide what you want and write it down nothing changes. What happens then if you take action to decide what you want, but take no action or inadequate action to execute your *Steps to Success*?

"The only free cheese is in the mouse trap."
- Russian Proverb

The results are the same. Nothing changes. You must take action before you receive the rewards.

Get Up, Get Moving And Fulfill Your Dreams!

To realize your goals, to accomplish great things, to reach peak performance, to gain the Winning Edge, you must first take action. I wish it were different, I wish that we could blink our eyes, wave a wand, or wiggle our noses and our dreams would come true. Unfortunately, it doesn't work that way.

Don't wait another moment! Taking action is the one key that unlocks all success. Just like Summer, and so many other successful people, you have tremendous power inside of you right now to change your life and live your dreams! I believe in you and I believe that you will make the five *PowerPrinciples* a force in your life. I'm excited for you because you have a marvelous future ahead of you. You are in the right place, at the right time, and nothing can stop you!

AFTERWORD

Jump!

> It was just at that moment when I heard the people on the ground start to chant, "Jump! Jump! Jump!'"

Jump!

I had no idea how long I'd been standing there but it seemed like an eternity. It was a cold, dark November evening and I was starting to shiver. My heart was pounding out of my chest. I tried to focus on my breathing and could see little clouds of mist each time I exhaled. Looking down again my head started to spin. From the top of the tower the people on the ground looked tiny. Behind me on the stairs I could hear the howls of laughter from my brothers egging me on. These were the same jokers who had convinced me that jumping off this tower with rubber bands attached to my ankles was a good idea.

My mind flashed back to how I had gotten myself in this predicament. My younger brothers had pushed the idea at dinner that evening and pride and ego had done the rest of the work. It was at that moment when I heard the spectators on the ground start to chant, "Jump! Jump! Jump!"

Frozen

My heart pounded as I just stood there frozen in fear. "Come on Jeb, you can do it," I said weakly to myself. How long had I been standing there? I couldn't get my bearings. All I wanted to do was walk back down those stairs, call it a day, and go back to the hotel.

Fear! I could feel it pulsing through my body. My stomach churned as I took another look down. I tried to move forward but my feet wouldn't budge. I could hear the crowd, "Jump! Jump! Jump!"

I tried to think about all of the other times in my

life when I'd taken a risk and just jumped. Was this moment any different than the first cold call I'd made or my first big presentation? How about the first time I held my son - that was fear!

This was a lot safer than the last hurricane I'd been through. I had a safety line, trained staff and a huge inflated cushion to catch my fall if all else failed. There had been a million moments in my life where I had to step out into the open, overcome fear, and jump with no safety net to catch my fall. Why was I so afraid?

The Unknown

Deep inside I knew the answer to that question. I was afraid because this was new - something I'd never experienced before. The unknown is frightening. The unknown holds us back from our dreams. Our fear keeps us from reaching for the things we want most in life. We are afraid we'll fall and fail. But it is when we are most afraid that we must will ourselves to move forward.

I looked back at my brothers. They were waiting and ready to pounce if I chickened out. There was no going back, staying put was not an option, and there was only one way down. At that moment I gathered up my fear, closed my eyes, and jumped...

What a ride!

Jeb Blount is a sought after speaker, trainer, and Professional Sales Coach, known for his ability to inspire others to action. As a business leader he has extensive experience turning around and righting troubled organizations. He has a passion for growing people and the unique ability to see potential in everyone. Over the span of his twenty year career he has coached, trained and developed hundreds of Sales Professionals, managers, and leaders.

Jeb has a core philosophy that in every endeavor in life, business, and sport, there are a handful of key principles, the basics, which, if focused on intently, will drive peak performance and achievement. He seeks to remove complexity from inherent business challenges, and instead focus individuals, leaders, and organizations on the core activities that will deliver quick and sustainable results.

He lives with his family in Cape Coral, Florida and Thomson, Georgia.

Jeb is a frequent guest lecturer at the University of Central Florida, a coach to the UCF National Collegiate Sales Competition team, publishes a popular weekly e-Zine, has a top ranked Podcast and is the founder of SalesGravy.com. He has shared his powerful message with groups as diverse as the NBA, Sonitrol, nutrisystem, the US Air Force, and La Petite Academy. To inquire about scheduling Jeb to speak to your group please send an email to cyndi@salesgravy.com or go to www. SalesGravy.com for more information.

ACKNOWLEDGEMENTS

I am blessed to have so many wonderful people in my life who have freely given their time, effort and emotions to help build this book. I pray that you feel my sincere, heart-felt, and enthusiastic thank you.

Jodi Bagwell, Jason Bagwell, Carrie Blount, Chris Dods, Larry Hake, Deborah Koch, you have shown incredible patience as you've read the pages of this book over and over again. It was your efforts that shaped and built this book layer by layer and page by page. PowerPrinciples is a reflection of your enthusiasm for success. You are amazing friends. Thank you!

Emily Campbell, thank you so much for your "non-sales" point of view. Because of your feedback PowerPrinciples grew and matured into a book for everyone. Brian Stanton, thank for your constant encouragement, awesome quote and for being a sounding board for all of the crazy ideas. Brenda White, thank you for being my cheerleader.

Lisa Bryant there are no words to thank you for keeping my spirits up and my eyes focused on the stars. You are a wonderful coach and a great friend. April Canada, thank you for your awesome feedback on chapter four. Mark McDaniel and TJ Freetage, thank you for the early feedback - you let me know that we were on the right track.

Nicole Howatt, thank you for setting this project in motion. You were the tipping point. Brad Sonday and Clay Hill, thank you for taking time to share your inspiring stories with me. You gave me courage to follow my dream. Jeff Lehman, Michelle Nichols, and Sherry Hines, thank you for showing me the ropes on writing and publishing.

Constance Dierickx, you changed my life. Thank you for teaching me to slow down and listen. Jebby Blount, thank you for making me feel like a million bucks every time you asked me if I was a writer.

Ed Evans, thank you for your help in creating a much better ending.

Bill Sutton, you opened big doors for me and Sales Gravy. I will never stop thanking you for your kindness.

David Stanfill and SayitontheWeb.com - you rock! Palm Tree Press, thanks for the sunshine.

Mom and Dee, thank you for the sacrifices you made to provide a happy and rewarding childhood and the resources to take advantage of life's opportunities. Lucy, Serena, PJ and Patrick thank you for your encouragement and support.

My Coaches:

All success is a result of great coaching. In your own way, you have each had a profound impact on my life. Thank you for investing your time, effort and emotion to help me become a better person.

Jodi Bagwell, Bob Blackwell, Jeff Black, Dee Campbell, Bill Carstens, Constance Dierickx, Paul Difucia, Chris Dods, Steve Donly, Joe Ernst, Ed Evans, Mary Gardner, Gary Glover, Larry Hake, Dale Holloway, Mitch Johnson, Jeff Lehman, Clarence Leonard, Chuck Mears, Matt McConaughy, Roger McKee, Clint Morris, Robert Ng, David Pannell, Bruce Polk, Jack Santos, Shirley Schumacher, Tom Siciliano, Brad Sonday, Brian Tracy, Elaine Tyler, Tom Vozzo, Brenda White, Jim Yamauchi

Ron and David, its time for a cold one. I'll see you at the Tiki Hut!